W9-BHF-687

GRAPHIC SCIENCE

DECODING GENES

WITH MAX AXIOM
SUPER SCIENTIST

by Amber J. Keyser, PhD

illustrated by Tod G. Smith and Al Milgrom

Consultant:
Monte Westerfield, PhD
Professor of Biology
University of Oregon

CAPSTONE PRESS
a capstone imprint

Graphic Library is published by Capstone Press,
151 Good Counsel Drive, P.O. Box 669, Mankato, Minnesota 56002.
www.capstonepress.com

092009
005619WZS10

Books published by Capstone Press are manufactured with paper
containing at least 10 percent post-consumer waste.

Library of Congress Cataloging-in-Publication Data
Keyser, Amber.
    Decoding genes with Max Axiom, super scientist / by Amber J. Keyser ; illustrated by
Tod G. Smith and Al Milgrom.
    p. cm.—(Graphic library. Graphic science.)
Summary: "In graphic novel format, follows the adventures of Max Axiom as he explains
    the science behind genes" — Provided by publisher.
    Includes bibliographical references and index.
    ISBN 978-1-4296-3976-7 (library binding)
    ISBN 978-1-4296-4862-2 (paperback)
    1. Genes — Comic books, strips, etc. — Juvenile literature. 2. DNA — Comic books,
strips, etc. — Juvenile literature. I. Smith, Tod, ill. II. Milgrom, A. (Allen), ill. III. Title.
QH447.K47 2010
576.5 — dc22   2009039894

Designer
Alison Thiele

Media Researcher
Wanda Winch

Cover Colorist
Krista Ward

Production Specialist
Laura Manthe

Colorist
Matt Webb

Editor
Mari Bolte

TABLE OF CONTENTS

Back in 1860, Gregor Mendel became the father of genetics.

Mendel crossed pea plants with different traits. Then he examined the offspring.

The experiments were simple but required careful counting and recording.

When I plant seeds from the yellow pods, the new plants also have yellow pods.

And the seeds from the green pods always make more green pods!

Each plant must have something inside that makes the right color.

In my time, we call that special something a gene.

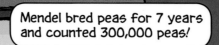

MENDEL'S FINDINGS

1. GENES MAKE PHENOTYPES.

2. EVERYONE HAS TWO COPIES OF EACH GENE, CALLED ALLELES.

3. ONE COPY COMES FROM EACH PARENT.

4. DOMINANT ALLELES HIDE RECESSIVE ONES.

Mendel bred peas for 7 years and counted 300,000 peas!

His findings are the basis of the science we call genetics.

Let's explore some human traits.

The allele for dimples is dominant to the allele for no dimples.

Can you guess which person has the allele for dimples?

They're held together by small molecules called bases.

There are four kinds of bases: adenine, guanine, thymine, and cytosine.

Bases pair up in a certain way. Adenine pairs with thymine. Guanine pairs with cytosine.

T
A
G
C
THYMINE
ADENINE
GUANINE
CYTOSINE

STRUCTURE OF DNA

In 1953, Francis Crick and James Watson discovered the structure of DNA. By doing this, they won a great scientific race to unravel the puzzle of heredity. Both later acknowledged that they couldn't have done it without Rosalind Franklin's help. She took a special picture of DNA using X-ray crystallography.

To recap, DNA is made of four chemical bases arranged in a double spiral. Sections of DNA, called genes, are code for proteins. Individual strands of DNA, called chromosomes, carry thousands of genes. All the strands of DNA together make up the genome, the body's entire genetic makeup.

The human genome contains more than 20,000 genes. They decide the makeup of skin, bone, brain, and muscle.

The average gene is 10,000 to 15,000 bases long.

Scientists determine the exact order of the bases of the genomes of many different organisms. This process is called sequencing.

By studying the genomes of many different organisms, scientists discovered an amazing fact. From fruit flies to humans, many of our genes are almost exactly the same.

HUMAN ATTGACG

CHIMP ACTAGCG

Powerful computers can compare genomes of different species. Ninety-six percent of human DNA is identical to chimpanzees.

That means humans and chimps are closely related.

The differences between our two species are caused by small differences in DNA.

16

Imagine that genes are like a deck of cards. Your mom got one set from each of her parents.

Your dad also got one set from each of his parents.

When they had you and your sister, they shuffled the genes. You each got your own set.

Gene shuffling is an important part of reproduction.

And it explains why we're all different.

Since the discovery of DNA, genetics has become an important aspect in the study of life.

Genetic discoveries have influenced conservation, medicine, and farming.

This new knowledge raises ethical questions too.

Should we use DNA from living creatures to make exact copies or clones?

And what happens when we put new genes into these corn plants?

They may produce more food, but would it be safe to eat?

26

MORE ABOUT GENES

Genotype is not the only thing that causes phenotype. Environment is important too. Even if a person has genes for being tall, without enough to eat, he'll be short.

The condition called Down syndrome occurs when a human child ends up with 47 chromosomes instead of 46.

To make Dolly, the famous sheep clone, scientists took a cell from an adult sheep and removed the DNA. They injected the DNA into an egg cell without any DNA. Then they put the egg inside of a female sheep where it grew into a new lamb. Dolly was an exact genetic copy of the first sheep.

Identical twins are a kind of clone. Very early in development, a fertilized egg splits in half. Each half grows into a baby. They are identical because each twin has exactly the same genes.

Many genes are necessary to tell cells when to divide and when to stop dividing. If a mutation occurs in any of those genes, cells will divide when they aren't supposed to. This results in the disease called cancer.

Genetic modification occurs when a scientist takes a gene from one organism and puts it into another. For example, a gene from bacteria was added to the corn genome. The gene makes a protein that kills caterpillars. The good thing is that farmers don't have to spray corn with insecticide. The bad thing is that the gene could spread to other plants and could even affect human health.

Some geneticists are trying to find cures for common genetic diseases using gene therapy. The idea is to replace damaged or mutated genes with normal ones.

 There are many kinds of genetics. Some geneticists study the genomes of endangered species. Others try to understand how each individual gene gives directions to the body. They may also study phenotypes like height that are caused by many genes working together. Still others use genes to understand how groups of plants and animals have changed over time.

MORE ABOUT

SUPER SCIENTIST

Real name: Maxwell J. Axiom
Hometown: Seattle, Washington
Height: 6' 1" **Weight:** 192 lbs
Eyes: Brown **Hair:** None

Super capabilities: Super intelligence; able to shrink to the size of an atom; sunglasses give x-ray vision; lab coat allows for travel through time and space.

Origin: Since birth, Max Axiom seemed destined for greatness. His mother, a marine biologist, taught her son about the mysteries of the sea. His father, a nuclear physicist and volunteer park ranger, schooled Max on the wonders of earth and sky.

One day on a wilderness hike, a megacharged lightning bolt struck Max with blinding fury. When he awoke, Max discovered a newfound energy and set out to learn as much about science as possible. He traveled the globe earning degrees in every aspect of the field. Upon his return, he was ready to share his knowledge and new identity with the world. He had become Max Axiom, Super Scientist.

allele (UH-lee-uhl) — one of two genes in a pair contributed by the parent

base (BAYS) — a building block of DNA; the four bases are adenine, guanine, thymine, and cytosine.

chromosome (KROH-muh-sohm) — a structure inside a cell containing genetic codes that control growth, development, and function of all cells

DNA (dee-en-AY) — the molecule that carries all of the instructions to make a living thing and keeps it working; short for deoxyribonucleic acid.

dominant (DOM-uh-nuhnt) — the gene most likely to produce a trait in offspring

gene (JEEN) — a part of every cell that carries physical and behavioral information passed from parents to their children

genetic mutation (juh-NET-ik myoo-TAY-shun) — a change in an animal's genetic makeup that causes it to develop in a different way

genotype (JEE-noh-tipe) — the genes that produce a phenotype

heredity (huh-RED-uh-tee) — the process by which parents pass traits to their children

nucleus (NOO-klee-uhss) — the part of each cell that contains the genetic material

phenotype (FEE-noh-tipe) — traits you can see, count, or measure

protein (PROH-teen) — a substance found in all living animal and plant cells; protein is necessary for growth and life.

recessive (ruh-SESS-iv) — the gene most likely to stay hidden in offspring

READ MORE

Hartman, Eve, and Wendy Meshbesher. *The Role of Genes*. Sci-Hi: Life Science. Chicago: Raintree, 2009.

Keyser, Amber. *The Basics of Cell Life with Max Axiom, Super Scientist*. Graphic Science. Mankato, Minn.: Capstone Press, 2010

Phelan, Glen. *Double Helix: The Quest to Uncover the Structure of DNA*. Science Quest. Washington, D.C.: National Geographic, 2006.

Simpson, Kathleen. *Genetics: From DNA to Designer Dogs*. National Geographic Investigates Science. Washington, D.C.: National Geographic, 2008.

Stille, Darlene. *Genetics: A Living Blueprint*. Exploring Science. Minneapolis: Compass Point Books, 2006.

INTERNET SITES

FactHound offers a safe, fun way to find Internet sites related to this book. All sites on FactHound have been researched by our staff.

Here's all you do:

Visit *www.facthound.com*

FactHound will fetch the best sites for you!